I0442094

# Mandala Wonders Coloring

*Copyright: Published in the United States Peter Raymond*
*Published April 2016*
*ISBN-13: 978-1530902286*
*ISBN-10: 1530902282*

# Thank you

www.ingramcontent.com/pod-product-compliance
Lightning Source LLC
Chambersburg PA
CBHW081555280526
45788CB00011B/3479
*9781530902286*